The Riddle of Correspondences in A. S. Byatt's *Possession: A Romance* with H. D.'s *Trilogy*

Unedited complete version of the paper
published Summer 2005 in
*Storytelling: A Critical Journal of
Popular Narrative*[i]

Written by Hedwig Gorski, Ph.D.

J A D Z I A

B O O K S

The Riddle of Correspondences in A. S. Byatt's Possession: A Romance with H. D.'s Trilogy © 2018 Hedwig Gorski

All rights reserved. This book may not be reproduced, in whole or in part, including photos and illustrations, in any form (beyond that copying permitted by Sections 107 and 108 of the U.S. Copyright Law and except by reviewers for the public press), without written permission from the copyright holders. Reviewers can use portions of the book contents, including images, in any medium with appropriate citations to discuss the book.

For information about this and other works by Hedwig Gorski, please contact: HGDGarts@gmail.com

Review and production requests to use the poems for performances, film, etc., are welcome. Mail/email:
> *HGDG Arts*
> 1053 McVeigh Road,
> Arnauldville, Louisiana, 70512, USA

Library of Congress Control Number:

> Publisher Cataloging Data
> Gorski, hedwig i.
> The riddle of correspondences in a. s. byatt's possession: a romance with h. d.'s trilogy
> 1. Literary Criticism

ISBN-13:
978-1725926462

ISBN-10:
1725926466
Literary Criticism; American

Women's Studies, Creative Criticism, British Women Novelists, American Modernism, Poetry, Hilda Doolittle

Cover Photo of Portia Munson's *The Garden* installation, 1996

"Please give my very best wishes to Hedwig Gorski whose analysis is a work of art."

A. S. Byatt, 7/28/2006

(from Ms. Byatt's email responding to *Storytelling* editors about "Riddle")

Preface

This article was first published in *Storytelling: A Critical Journal of Popular Narrative,* Summer 2005, in edited form. Several pages of detailed comparisons with the images used by American poet H. D. and Byatt's novel were removed by *Storytelling* editors due to article length issues. This monograph includes all pages of analysis written by Dr. Gorski for those who want to enjoy the *creative literary criticism* develop strengthening the author's radical yet seemingly undeniable conclusions. After its publication, the author A. S. Byatt sent an email note to the journal acknowledging Gorski's analysis as a "work of art." Gorski read Byatt's note as a double entendre because of her creative analytical thesis approach in conjunction with the nature of Byatt's *academic detective* novel. Gorski's first interpretation of the note was at face value. Secondly, Gorski immediately thought of Plato's attitude toward *art* as secondary re-creations of the truth and delighted in Byatt's approval and understanding of the article with the double entendre she inferred from the note.

Gorski acknowledges this article is "creative" literary criticism. Creative literary criticism, according Gorski, presents a highly unique premise about a literary work that may seem difficult to prove, one that may seem a bit fantastical until it is proven with undeniable factual evidence within the article discussion. "The greatest works in literature were often created in a playful trance or whimsy which permitted free creative invention untethered by expectations pre-existing in the status quo," she stated. *Creative literary criticism* can follow suit by proving more playful theories with solid evidence that can't be denied convincing readers of its validity. After reading this monograph, readers can decide if the ubiquitous correspondences between the two works result from H. D.'s significant conscious or unconscious influence upon Byatt or represent a set of universal feminine and feminist symbols that exist in a Jungian collective unconscious female mind.

Abstract

The Riddle of Correspondences in A. S. Byatt's *Possession: A Romance* with H. D.'s *Trilogy*

Confluences between A.S. Byatt's Poe-like narrative, *Possession: A Romance*, with H. D.'s *Trilogy* prove too tempting to ignore. The paper unravels textual clues proposing Byatt's unique solution for the ultimate goal of a realistic novel, blurring reality and fiction, which also provides the novel's readers with an actual literary mystery to uncover.

The Riddle of Correspondences in A. S. Byatt's *Possession: A Romance* with H. D.'s *Trilogy*

Scholars uncovering the literary allusions in A. S. Byatt's postmodern novel *Possession A Romance* have formed a list of authors which constitute the rich literary confluence in the work; a list that is, undoubtedly, incomplete. Byatt's expansive knowledge of "literary, literary-critical, philosophical, scientific, psychological" (Kelly vii) texts would preclude the impossibility of an exhaustive tracing of influences so soon after *Possession's* 1990 publishing date. Kathleen Coyne Kelly's *A. S. Byatt*[ii] suggests Iris Murdoch, George Eliot, and Honore de Balzac as Byatt's "models" for her realistic fiction with composites of Emily Dickenson, Christina Rossetti, Elizabeth Barrett Browning, Wordsworth, Carlyle, to name a few[iii], for the characters. Her refracted characters exist within both the Victorian sensibility and the contemporary academic politics that form the novel's dualistic ambience. She uses invented literature, a para-literature that form's the oeuvres of the fictional writers, and fictitious epistolary texts that, at once, become the artifacts of fictional fact and the cryptogram that hints at an authorial riddle. If in the deepest layers of parchment, the reader detects the faintest ghosts of a text or an author underneath the explicit literary corollaries, is not the reader then obligated to unravel the mystery by assuming textual inferences in order to enhance faint impressions toward legibility? There is a portrait of a twentieth-century "poetess" in *Possession* that remains the exclusive possession of, if not Byatt, the novel itself, until the reader discovers that the novel is a real artifact of clues to solve the riddle it contains: that A. S. Byatt's *Possession A Romance* contains unmistakably pointed correspondences to American modernist poet H. D. (Hilda Doolittle) and her epic *Trilogy*. A juxtaposition of the corresponding evidence may help to uncover a conscious effort by Byatt to embed the clues and riddle of H. D. allusions into her novel to give the reader an actual experience in the reality of scholarly discovery while reading about similar activity by fictional scholars in the novel.

Possession crosses the threshold[iv] between a mimetic representation about the obsessive competition in the communal effort of literary scholarship to a "knowing postmodern vision," as Kelly calls it, that may be a conscious or unconscious solution to Byatt's concern with the reader's experience. Kelly writes: "A postmodern novel asks us to stop believing in a distinction between fiction and reality. . . . [and is] big enough for multiple and conflicting interpretations" (xii). Postmodern criticism necessitates a "free play of mind" (Kelly xi) to deal with a contemporary aesthetic that tries to blur divisions between truth and fiction. Byatt admits a belief in the relevancy of the past to present-day readers evident in *Possession*'s temporal congruencies, which serve to educate the uninitiated reader about the literary past[v] through investigations by twentieth-century scholars, a plot that is an entertaining and accessible mystery-romance as well as a how-to manual for arm-chair scholars. This paper argues that Byatt has included a real textual mystery to unravel within the text of *Possession* creating an intriguing postmodern solution for the problem of achieving the ultimate goal of a realistic novel. Kelly reminds us

Byatt agrees with Elizabeth Bowen's opinion that the objective of a novel in its complex relations of truth and fiction is the "non-poetic statement of a poetic truth" (13). The novel's "trail of clues . . . often entails unraveling obscure allusions" concerned (on numerous superimposed levels) with female vision, art, and thought (79).

A number of biographical coincidences between H. D. and Byatt tied to textual clues indicate that H. D. may be one of the obscure allusions in *Possession*. Byatt announces that there is, first of all, a mystery to be solved by using the word "purloined" to describe Roland's theft[vi] of significant letters that uncover a mysterious romantic liaison. Edgar Allen Poe's purloined letter also reveals an illicit romance. Like readers of Edgar Allen Poe's "The Purloined Letter," *Possession* readers must wait for their fictional characters to solve the riddle in order to unravel the fictional mystery. The obvious literary allusion to Poe could not have been coincidental to Byatt's design[vii]. She proclaims herself a "greedy reader"[viii] intimating her probable knowledge of H. D.'s oeuvre, particularly since she entered the Somerville College of Oxford University in 1958, a decade after H. D.'s *Trilogy* was published by the Oxford University Press, and after attending Bryn Mawr College during 1957-58 where H. D. was educated during 1905. Two years before *Possession* was published, a revival of interest in H. D. included an *Agenda* special issue dedicated to H. D. funded by the London Art Council and published in London during 1988. Byatt's repeated use of the word "palimpsest" in *Possession* implies that Byatt knew of H. D.'s novel *Palimpsest*, reported to be a mixture of poetry and prose like *Possession*. Byatt's repeated use of the word "purloined" with "letter" implies Poe's mystery just as Byatt's repeated use of the word "palimpsest" in connection with women's literature infers a greedy reader's awareness of H. D.'s novel and the word's significance in *Trilogy*.

"The Correspondence," an epistolary chapter in *Possession*, reveals a romance between two fictional nineteenth-century poets, Christabel LaMotte and Randolph Henry Ash, who describes reality as obscured by a "piling up [of] speculation and observations until truths . . . graspable in the bright Dayspring of human morning are now obscured by palimpsest on palimpsest" (181). Speculations about which literary figures Christabel and Ash represent have excluded, to my knowledge, any consideration that Christabel could be a nineteenth century version of H. D. and her correspondence to Ash a partial allusion to H. D.'s lifelong correspondence with Ezra Pound[ix]. Both female poets, the fictional Christabel and H. D., express the interest in writing an epic poem and how that goal equates to patriarchal society during their respective time periods. H. D. credits Pound's *Cantos*[x] as a model for her epic *Trilogy*, and Ash, like Pound with H. D., encourages Christabel to write one.

Correspondence between Blanche Glover and Ellen Ash, Randolph's wife, points to similar triads in the relationships surrounding the fictional Christabel and H. D., both of whom may have had lesbian relationships with their live-in female companions, Christabel with the painter Blanche Glover and H. D. with Bryher Macpherson, H. D.'s companion of forty years. Like Christabel, H. D. gave birth to one child, a daughter named Perdita in 1919, after the stillbirth of her first child in 1915. In "A Postlude" to her novel *HERmione*, H. D. writes that Pound did not visit her when she lost her first child but did "hurtle[s] himself into the decorous St. Faith's Nursing Home. . . . pounding" the wall with an ebony walking stick. He expresses regrets that the second child was not his; one could infer that the first stillborn child must have been his (<u>HERmione</u> 237). The baby girl named Perdita after the lost daughter of Queen Hermione in Shakespeare's *The Winter's Tale* reflected the first stillborn child as that which was lost and found again with the birth of Frances Perdita Aldington[xi] (Guest 110-11). Bryher nursed the pregnant H. D. to health after moving her to the nursing home where Dorothy Shakespeare (Pound's wife) gave the child a coral bracelet with obliging acceptance of the triadic relationship. Byatt's triadic relationships in *Possession* mirror H. D.'s life as much, or more, than the accepted real-life analogs of triadic relationships between Wordsworth and Annette Vallon or Christina Rossetti and W. B. Scott, as suggested by reviewer Michael Dirda according to Kelly (81).

The greatest indication of Byatt's use of the Pound/H. D. relationship as one analog, perhaps the major one, for the Ash/LaMotte triangle in *Possession* is Byatt's structure of the meeting between Ash and LaMotte's daughter Maia into a brief segment at the end of *Possession*, "Postcript 1868," strikingly similar to the conclusion of HERmione, "A Postlude," described above. Speculations about LaMotte's child being stillborn and the ill effects of the pregnancy on LaMotte as described in Sabine's fictional journal mirror H. D.'s pregnancies. Sabine, a cousin with whom the pregnant LaMotte stays, describes Christabel's mysterious disappearance from Sabine's home and an even more mysterious return without her baby, purportedly stillborn. She portrays Christabel as gaunt and ill in the same way H. D. must have looked to Bryher when she found H. D. near death with pneumonia shortly before Perdita's birth. In "Postscript 1868," Byatt reveals that the supposed stillborn child of poets Randolph Henry Ash and Christabel LaMotte survived and was named Maia after the mother of Hermes[xii]. Like H. D.'s "Postlude" to her novel <u>HERrmione</u>, Byatt's "Postscript" describes Ash's meeting with his assumed daughter who calls herself May a simplification of Maia.

    The reader must solve the actual mystery in the manner used by the fictional scholars, Roland and Maud, to solve the fictional mystery. Roland and Maud compare fictional actual texts (letters and journals for biographical information) to actual fictional texts (poems by the fictional poets in the novel) the way the reader of *Possession* must zig-zag between reality (critical reading of a novel) and the fictionalized realities in the novel. Maud explains her research to Sir and Lady Bailey who mistake her interest in writing about Christabel:

> "Ah," said Lady Bailey. "A biography. How interesting.
> I don't see," said Sir George, "that there'd be much to put in a biography. She didn't <u>do</u> anything. Just lived up there in the east wing and poured out all this stuff about fairies. It wasn't a <u>life</u>." (89)

Maud's reply that she is writing a critical

study rather than a biography displeases Sir George because it is a reminder of the supposed feminists' intrusion in the upkeep of Christabel's grave. Later, the scholars dig up Ellen Ash's grave to retrieve the buried secret letters. The actual riddle Byatt hides under the fictional text may remain buried unless it is brought to the surface of the palimpsest for a critical paper like this one. In addition to the vertical zig zag through the layers of the palimpsest, there is a horizontal zig zagging through time for the fictional scholars and the reader, who must negotiate between fiction and reality. The result is a three-dimensional mise-en-abime which is the exclusive property in reality of the reader Byatt describes in "Reading": "somewhere, somehow, there might be someone on the lookout for the subtleties which you couldn't expect everyone to understand" (qtd. in *A. S. Byatt* 15). This reader, then, the one who possesses the awareness of the riddle of correspondence between *Possession* and Trilogy becomes a matrix for the multiple meanings of the word "correspondence"[xiii] in addition to the word "possession."

Possession contains a corresponding responsibility that involves risk. Maud is threatened by Roland's possession of Christabel's letters and by letters from other scholars, Leonora Stern and Fergus Wolf, following the same trail of correspondence that "alarms" Maud. In the letter that Maud reads in the safety of her apartment, Christabel informs Ash that there is a riddle to solve while it confirms to the reader that there is another riddle contained within:

> Here is . . . an old Riddle, an easy Riddle . . . a fragile riddle, in white and Gold with life in the middle of it. . . . let it slip through your mind's

> fingers. . . . lies inside Alabaster. . . .
> no lid you may lift . . . for all is
> sealed and smooth. (152)

This letter is written with the characteristic dash punctuation that Roland notes is part of Christabel's signature style of writing and offers another undeniable link to H. D., whose prose in *Palimpsest* and other texts is abundantly punctuated with dashes[xiv]. Correspondence between reality and fiction for the reader aware of both texts and suspicious of Byatt's designs must read both texts simultaneously to uncover the real mystery in the artifice of both texts, which exists only in the correspondence of artifice to artifice, proven with facts that evidence Byatt's awareness of H. D.'s text.

Trilogy was published in the 1970s and has been kept in print due to the efforts of feminist scholars but is considered a relatively obscure major work by a debatably major modernist poet with an avant-garde propensity toward inter-genre explorations that included film as well as novels. Byatt must have been aware of *Trilogy* as explained in the factual biographical links discussed earlier. The Oxford University Press published separately the books that combined to form *Trilogy: The Walls Do Not Fall* in 1944; *Tribute to the Angels* in 1945; and, *The Flowering of the Rod* in 1946. One of the major themes in *Trilogy*, the sacred imagery of biblical women--how these images define the reality of patriarchy for ordinary women--is secularized in the fantastical fairy poetry of Christabel, the Victorian woman poet contrasted in the novel to the emergence of women scholars in the present who control the availability of women's literature/self-imaging.

    The juxtaposition of these two texts

evidences ironic correlations to women authors and women scholars: women must author their own images if they are to obtain authority in their lives and they need a support network to distribute the self-authored images. In order to do both, patriarchal authority must be disrupted making the upheaval of secrets buried under the patriarchal imagery of women a necessary political and aesthetic act. The disruption is echoed in Sir Bailey's fears of the scholars who threaten to revise his family's biographic history while they probe into Christabel's writing for critical study trying to establish her amongst the canon of male writers represented by Randolph Henry Ash. The male scholars in *Possession* are interested in Christabel's letters, however, because of her relationship to their primary literary concern, Ash's poetry and not Christabel's. Byatt's novel implies that women scholars are as crucial to women's literature as are the women authors of literature in accomplishing the aesthetic re-imaging of women in art resulting in the re-figuration of women in society. Recognition of H. D.'s significance to twentieth-century literature has been neglected or underestimated, even subordinated to her close relationship with Ezra Pound, until feminist scholars have re-invigorated the work with the autonomy and value it deserves. H. D., like Christabel, battled the Victorian social constraints that would lock women into "a glass coffin" in dead silence so that men could gaze at their beauty without threat of any kind. Women's texts buried under male authority and authorship go to the grave, as did the letters buried with Ellen Ash in *Possession*.

The re-imaging of late twentieth-century women in *Possession*'s hierarchy of scholars leaves Roland Michell in a position that mirrors a common dynamic encountered by women artists and scholars. Roland begins at the bottom of the hierarchy because his peers view him as inconsequential. The discovery of letters about which the major scholars know nothing presents an opportunity for the underdog protagonist who can keep the materials secret so that he can receive the credit for a new contribution to literary discourse, consequently elevating his status. However, it is his academic confidante in this venture, Maud, who helps Roland not as a woman-enabler like Ellen Ash, but like the man with higher status who helps a female colleague through the door of patriarchy. Maud escorts Roland to a higher status and not the opposite. Roland is the thief of the purloined letters produced by Maud's ancestors following a matrilineal path to

Christabel. Roland gives up Val, his girlfriend, and must leave home to follow Maud in their research: another so-called woman's scenario where she foregoes having children or marrying for the sake of a successful career. This gender reversal of stereotypical roles in *Possession* finds a correspondence in its predecessor *Trilogy*.

In the third book of Trilogy, "The Flowering of the Rod," a passive outsider who witnesses Mary Magdala's heroic gesture, does not prevent it nor facilitate it. The male witness, Kaspar, observes, and the poem's record of his observations underscores the official biblical story of Mary Magdala washing Jesus's feet with her tears and drying it with her hair. The addition of Kaspar's witnessing initiates a query about what he is witnessing while lending a synecdoche of male validation to the vision of Our Lady experienced by

Kaspar. The reader of the poem must supply the answer to the riddle of Kaspar's vision in order to experience an epiphany about the meaning of the poem. What occurs in Kaspar's vision is the alchemical result of the poet as pagan priestess in the act of conjuring herself into a powerful conflated image of Our Lady and human Woman. Alicia Ostriker tributes H. D. with writing "something like a new Gnostic Gospel, fusing the persons of the virgin-mother and the Magdelene and delicately proposing an ultimately matriarchal base for all western culture" (50). The poem extends the conflations to Kaspar with other male figures in the poem as a correlating necessity for the success of a reified image of Woman based on the conflated Mary's.

The act of acquiring power and status through the art of superimposing images is one method H. D. uses to control

the definition and meaning attached to
ordinary women through sacred images and
art. In "The Flowering of the Rod," the
poet's effectiveness as prophet can be
measured from a historical-political feminist
perspective. The biblical dichotomy
represented by Mary, the Mother of God,
and Mary Magdala was attacked by early
feminists because of their patriarchal
stereotypes negating the whole women. In
section 9, H. D. informs the reader that she
is real and natural acting as
poet/prophet/priestess to actualize feminine
power:

>No poetic fantasy
>but biological reality,
>
>a fact: I am an entity like
>bird, insect, plan
>
>or sea-plant cell;

I live; I am alive; (125)

She replaces images associated with male construction and destruction, a "pyramid," "fallen cities," and "a heap of skulls" (Golgotha) with feminine images of creation, a "lily" blooming and unfolding its petals to show the "flower-cone" and "seed" that will flower despite the destruction and decay of Man's world. The conflation of fragmented patriarchal images of women like the biblical Mary's begins with a superimposition of women's sacred images upon the male power structure and acquires solidity by the overlay of the female images, one upon the other, which becomes a confirmation of H. D.'s power as a real woman and poet in the role of conjurer/artist/priestess ordained to transubstantiate "the new wine" into a blooded reality.

    H. D. begins the conflation of

biblical Mary's in section 12 by confusing Mary of Bethany with Mary Magdala, the first "reviled" for "having left home / and not caring for house-work" and seen by society as "unbalanced, neurotic"; the second known as a sinner. Mary Magdala convinces Kaspar to give her his alabaster jar[xv] of myrrh by her unexpected behavior:

> she simply didn't care whether he acclaimed
> or snubbed her or worse; what are insults?
>
> she knew how to detach herself,
> another unforgivable sin,
>
> and when the stones were hurled,
> she simply wasn't there; (130-31)

As Mary Magdala stands "planted" inside Kaspar's doorway, she wills herself to become myrrh through her power to superimpose upon her own the images of the "Mary's a-plenty": though I am "Mara, bitter" (sinner) "I shall be Mary-myrrh" (Holy Mary). In section 17, the holiness of the latter overlays the former in Kaspar's doorway as mysterious light that satisfies his vision like a mirage of fresh water sustained by "a parched, dying man, lost in the desert. . ."[xvi] (136). Both dichotomous Mary's announce themselves in the single glowing figure of Kaspar's vision in section 19:

> *I am Mary, the incense flower of the incense-tree,*
>
> *myself worshiping, weeping, shall be changed to myrrh*[xvii] *(138)*

Here the Mother Mary's pain at the foot of the cross is superimposed upon Mary Magdala's weeping at Jesus's feet in Simon's house. The dialogue that followed is the voice of Mary Magdala, "though melted away" from the sinner imaged earlier; she retains her human woman power symbolized by the tower in Magdala, also a symbol of earthly place, autonomy, and used like the cliché "a tower of strength." The poem ends with Kaspar's memory of Mother Mary, to whom he gave a jar of myrrh ointment with the other Magi, superimposed upon the reader's memory of Mary Magdala's will toward transformation into myrrh, which has been accomplished as the poet narrator confirms the ultimate reification of Woman witnessed by Kaspar.

Kaspar's passive witnessing presents a distinct corollary to Roland in Byatt's *Possession*. Like Kaspar, Roland is an outsider humbled by his peers also benefiting through unexpected good fortune coupled with his ability to recognize its significance. Maud becomes an avatar of H. D.'s alchemy of conflated images as the beneficiary of the political empowerment prefigured in *Trilogy*. In addition to Roland's peculiar witnessing of Maud's inheritance of the artifacts he uncovered, which is similar to Kaspar's vision uncovering a re-figuring of Woman that Maud also inherits, numerous textual clues in *Possession* indicate Byatt's calculated correspondence of the Maud/Roland relationship to the Kaspar/Mary sequence. Byatt mirrors H. D.'s use of two significant tropes in relation to the heroine, the veil and hair, as seen through the eyes of the male protagonists, Roland and Kaspar.

Maude's green scarf is an analog to Mother Mary's blue mantel and Mary Magdala's veil. The scarf covers her blonde hair like a mantle while they discuss Christabel's insect poems in the Bailey mansion. Later, Maud and Roland retrace a trip to Whitby made a century earlier by Christabel and Ash and a shopkeeper admires Maud's antique green scarf which changes, Roland notices, to a more modern green and white checked scarf again covering her blonde hair. Roland connects Maud's comment "Celibacy is the new . . . indulgence" to the implied modesty of Maud's covered hair. He asks her to unpin her hair, a "captive creature," and watches her un-plait the long, thick braids as "a whirling light rush[ed] towards it and glitter[ed] on it" causing Roland to feel as if "something had been loosed in himself" (296). In *Trilogy*, Mary Magdala "deftly unweaving / the long, carefully-braided tresses / of her extraordinary hair" at Jesus's feet disarmed Simon as it did Kaspar earlier, who "saw the light on her hair / like moonlight on a lost river" (148). Connections between virginity and the Holy Mary's mantel, celibacy and Maud un-plaiting her hair, Mary Magdala's shameless "heathen" demonstration drying Jesus's feet with her hair resulting in a cleansing of her sins are similar analogs used by both authors with a variety of water/woman images.

In *Trilogy*, the sight of Mary Magdala at Jesus's feet reminds Simon of a Aheathen picture / or a carved stone-portal entrance / to a forbidden sea-temple; / they called the creature / depicted like this, seated on the sea-shore / or on a rock, a Siren, / a maid-of-the-sea, a mermaid" (142). Maud sitting by the Yorkshire cliffs and seashore in *Possession* is described through Roland's Kaspar-like vision. "The Fairy Melusine," Christabel's fairy poem, emphasizes the water/woman trope that caps veil/scarf/hair/celibacy sequences in H. D.'s epic as well as Byatt's novel. Raimondin passes a "still and secret pool" where Melusine sits with Aliving hair . . . brighter than chill gold . . . straying out to lighten the dun air / Like phosphorescent sparks off a pale sea" (321). Simon's reference to a forbidden sea-temple echoes H. D.'s reference to Atlantis in *Trilogy* corresponding directly to Christabel's poem "Drowned City of Is."

Christabel's cousin Sabine describes the legend of the City of Is providing a water/woman correspondence similar to H. D.'s use of Atlantis, a legendary city submerged under the ocean after an earthquake, as an echo of Simon's fear about Mary Magdala's autonomy in "The Flowering of the Rod." Sabine reads a description of Is that describes the legendary city as containing the:

> terror of ancient pagan cults and the
> terror of the passion of
> the senses, let loose in women. And
> to these two terrors is added
> the third, that of the Ocean. . . .

> Paganism, woman and the Ocean,
> these three desires and these three
> great fears of men are mingled
> in this strange legend and come to a
> tempestuous and terrible end. (370)

Sabine questions why desire and senses in women should terrify men and why the male author images women as witches, outcasts, monsters when describing what could be the "vestigal memory of an other world where women were powerful" (370). Sabine goes on to describe Christabel's ideal of a place "where women can be free to express their true natures" which have been divided in half by men:

> [Christabel] said, in Romance, women's two natures can be reconciled. I asked, which two natures, and she said, men saw women as double beings, enchantress and demons or innocent

angels. (404)

H. D. describes the instinctual longing for this separation in woman's nature to be united as the instinctual flight of "blue-geese, white-geese" (118) to the land where she belongs, is loved and loves, and is natural as rain (115). Woman's frustration discussed in Sabine's journals is part of the eternal urge for fulfillment, a heroic flight from limiting patriarchal stereotypes that becomes a migration to a drowned city which, nevertheless, satisfies the thirst of the geese who "drop / one by one, / for they fall exhausted, numb, blind / but in certain ecstacy" (120).

Trilogy is a poetics of conflations and superimpositions which are the "alchemist's secret Key" (40) to unlock the "sub-conscious ocean" "when identity would merge with the best," and "illusion, reversion of old values, / oneness lost, madness [Woman's wildness-naturalness]" would rise from the sea floor (41). H. D. jumps in time to gather the various precious jewels for the crown on woman's loosed hair[xviii] in her "age of new dimension" that is a "present" resulting from "dispersed mind, dared occult lore," into "a fine distillation of emotion" (40). Like Byatt's women in *Possession*, who create, select, re-instate, salvage, cherish, validate texts by women because they draw layer upon layer of corrected imagery empowering the community of Woman, H. D. uses her power as "scribe, second only to the pharaoh" to re-figure existing images into a truthful portrait of real women by gathering them into her alchemist's chalice and mixing them with personal symbols that have empowered her for transubstantiation. The benefits of the authentically drawn sacred images of women will fall like golden pollen, like manna, to nourish ordinary women whose power and autonomy are limited by patriarchal stereotypes. The "philosopher's stone / is yours if you surrender / sterile logic, trivial reason" (40). Disorienting sudden jumps between time periods during the Kaspar/memory/Mary-vision sequences that occur without preparation or explanation in *Trilogy* help in the conflation of the Virgin Mary with prostitute Mary into a whole image of Woman made of the two halves. Byatt uses the same technique[xix] in *Possession*.

    Byatt uses the seamless time jump to superimpose the nineteenth-century LaMotte/Ash narrative onto the narrative of the present-day relationship between Maud and Roland. Certain uncomfortably lengthy passages can be read as belonging in either century until Byatt provides a definite clue, the eventual naming of the characters who are speaking, to inform the reader which couple, the Victorian or the contemporary, is described in the scene[xx]. This reader-disorienting technique indicates Byatt's authorial playfulness with her reader illustrating an authorial propensity that supports the possibility of an included actual riddle for the reader to solveBthe implied connection to H.D. and *Trilogy*. Both texts use seamless time jumps as textual clues of association providing evidential support to further connect the specific texts by Byatt and H. D. to each other.

The omniscient narrator in *Possession* seems to be speaking directly to the reader at discreet points in the novel to encourage the reader's building suspicions that there is an actual mystery for him/her to solve. A parenthetical comparison of Blackadder's speculative thinking with that of the subject's, "(This was a very Ash-like speculation.)," leading to the innuendo of Roland's announcement about the purloined letters: "I think I made a discovery" (33-34), indicates there is a discovery to be made by the reader. Christabel writes to Ash in a letter: "imagine away; think what you will, and I shall from time to time write a small Clue, so that you may be more thoroughly confounded" (196). In another letter, Christabel asks:

> --oh but I am a mere poet; if I urge
> that we receive Truth only
> through the Life, or Liveliness, of
> Lie, there's no harm in that—
> since we all take in both with our
> mother-milk; Indissoluble it
> is the human case. (186)

Christabel continues by magnifying the power of ancient poets, the way H. D. does in *Trilogy*, through Christabel: "What a poet was then: seer, daemon, force of nature, the Word" (186). In the letter containing that statement, Christabel confesses that she is "threatened in that Autonomy for which I have so struggled." The threat is a shadow of H. D.'s birds risking free flight to drown in the ocean where Atlantis has disappeared. The *Possession* author/narrator seems to taunt the reader by Maud's considerations of Lacan's perception that "the grammatical subject of a statement differs from the subject, the 'I,' who is the object discussed," which leads Maud to wonder if her own thoughts are original and concluding that they were not because she is "A matrix for a susurration of texts and codes" (172-73), just as Byatt is as the author of *Possession*. This passage where Maud and Roland relate textual disclosure to discovering real truth concludes with the seeming transposition of a textual directive between the fictional characters to an authorial directive to the reader: "we'd better start looking for facts as well as images" (277).

This paper begins with factual biographical material that connects the two authors, H. D. and Byatt, in order to link the two texts *Trilogy* and *Possession* so as not to exclude the possibility of the thesis it supports. The case is strengthened with numerous correlations of factual material to the texts, such as the overuse of dash punctuation in H. D.'s *Palimpsest* and other novels and Christabel's prose. The correspondences of themes, images, tropes, associations, and writing techniques are too numerous for exhaustive discussion within the scope of this paper. Once the idea that Byatt did construct a built-in mystery for the reader to solve in connection with H. D.'s *Trilogy* is directed in a search for textual clues, the echoing between the two texts intensifies rather than diminishes. However, for the sake of increasing validation for my own speculation as stated in the thesis of this paper, it may be wise to briefly consider alternative reasons for the proliferation of textual echoes between the two texts. The most obvious alternative to intentional correspondence by Byatt to *Trilogy* is the notion that the myriad of echoing images and writing styles are coincidental, a Jungian synergy, or a Freudian confluence of feminine language.

Byatt presents the Freudian alternative in *Possession* with a comparison of female writing to Athe successive shivering delights of the female orgasm@ relating it to the form of Virginia Woolf's sentences and utterances, Charlotte Bronte's union with the power of the sea, and other correspondences contained in the fictional scholar Leonora Stern's fictional book on

Motif and Matrix in the Poems of LaMotte (265-67). However, an observation of the particulars of the textual correspondences between *Possession* and *Trilogy* contained in the word play of two specific instances negates an accidental or Freudian relationship. First, the Mary, mer, Maia, myrhh sequence and, second, the Osirius sequence originating in *Trilogy* and continued in *Possession*.

During a dinner scene in *Possession*, three fictional scholars discuss the whereabouts of Christabel and Ash's child. Cropper orders "lavishly, a huge platter [a metal pedestal] of fruits de mer" leaving behind a pile of shells and inedible "debris" from which "every sweet white morsel" had been extracted. The meal ends with several toasts to the child of Christabel and Ash beginning with the word "May" after Cropper announces his determination to uncover the secrets of the correspondence (letters) buried in the grave regarding the existence of the illegitimate child (463). Byatt reveals that Christabel's child, named Maia (472), was left in the care of her sister, Sophia[xxi], with a will to insure her possessions would be inherited by Maia, who, remember, simplified her name to May. Christabel's possessions were passed down to Maud, because of "the importance of handing things on through the female line[xxii]" (*Possession* 471). H. D.'s wordplay in I makes a comparison unavoidable:

> a word most bitter, *marah*,
> a word bitterer still, *mar*,
>
> sea, brine, breaker, seducer,
> giver of life, giver of tears;
>
> Now polish the crucible
> and set the jet of flame

> under, till *marah-mar*
> are melted, fuse and join
>
> and change and alter,
> mer, mere, mere, mater, Maia, Mary,
>
> Star of the Sea,
> Mother. (71)

H. D. connects the flowering of the rod with spring, May flowering, and the may-tree with "our jewel in the crucible" which is also "delicate, green-white, opalescent" (80). As mentioned earlier, Byatt associates the colors green and white with Maud, echoing the blue and white mantel of Mother Mary, which echoes the Queen of the Drowned City, and so forth. H. D.'s wordplay[xxiii] with Osiris is similar to that illustrated above and carried through in *Trilogy* as a reflection of the balancing male

47

element that evolves into Kaspar, as discussed earlier, who is conflated further with ancient mythical figures and male gods, in a wordplay of names for stars, constellations, and with Isis. The isolation of the syllable "is" in H. D.'s wordplay is mirrored by Byatt's use of the name "Is" in *Possession*.

The notes gloss additional word[xxiv] correspondences from the two texts that may help to prove the thesis this paper introduces. The connection the thesis initiates opens Byatt's greedy reading and lush writing for deeper critical examination; and, more importantly, calls for a more exhaustive critical evaluation of H.D.'s poetry and novels, a literary oeuvre that foreshadows postmodern aesthetics and feminist politics and which should not be erased from the palimpsest containing the female line. The conclusion to the mysterious web of confluences to H. D.'s *Trilogy* that Byatt seems to have woven into the fabric of *Possession* may be that romantic notion of loyalty as applied to her literary female line without subscribing to a "feminist programme" (qtd. in Kelly 12), freeing her to broaden gender issues into a realism that "capture[s] the complexity of human relations" (Kelly 8).

Perhaps the H. D. oeuvre after Imagism has been largely ignored because of its broad treatment of gender relations: too confusingly heterosexual and metaphysical for the male modernist canon and too grateful to famous male enablers for a wholehearted feminist restoration. Susan Friedman describes H. D.'s undeserved obscurity, particularly of her longer works like *Trilogy*, as "buried under a scattered knowledge of "Oread" or "Heat" and other short Imagist icons (47). If Byatt's novel

Possession A Romance appeared in the 1940s, it would undoubtedly be prophetic of a future feminist politic yet irrelevant to the consciousness of mid-century America or Europe. If it appeared in the early 1960s, it might be dismissed for its under-developed feminist party line; in the 1970s for an obsessive retrofit of Victorian sensibility (which has a renewed attraction for the AIDS-aware society of the 1990s). Like H. D., Byatt's agenda is aesthetic rather than political, but her work is less dependent on feminist scholars for critical study than H. D.'s. Byatt may have chosen a postmodern strategy to blur distinctions between art and life by including a built-in mystery for a reader familiar with *Trilogy* to solve. The final alternative to the notion introduced in this paper is that, contrary to Byatt's stated intentions to avoid an overpowering by any one "particular writer or system" (Kelly 7),

Byatt has unconsciously built in a literary allusion that belongs exclusively to the reader and exists exclusively in critical study. The alternative to the premise of intentionality suggests a gender-based Jungian collective unconscious filled with symbols, universal images, and metaphors specific to the female mind. This idea, too, would prove a fulfilling research endeavor in connection to motivating factors for transgenderism. Nevertheless, the volume of exacting correspondences between the two primary texts points to a conscious effort on the part of A. S. Byatt, one that playfully includes a riddle for the initiated reader to discover. The uncovering of the H. D. allusions becomes an additional conveyance of delight woven into the fabric of her realistic novel.

Works Cited

Byatt, A. S. *Possession A Romance*. New York: Vintage, 1990.

Friedman, Susan. "Who Buried H.D.? A Poet, Her Critics, and Her Place in The Literary Tradition." *Modern Critical Views: H. D.* Ed. Harold Bloom. New York: Chelsea House, 1989. 45-62.

Guest, Barbara. *Herself Defined: The Poet H.D. and Her World*. New York: Quill, 1984.

Hardin, Michael. AH.D.'s *Trilogy*: *Speaking Through the Margins*. Sagetrieb. 15.1-2 (1996): 151-159.

H. D. *HERmione*. New York: New Directions, 1981.

---. *Trilogy*. New York: New Directions, 1973.

Kelly, Kathleen Coyne. *A. S. Byatt*. New York: Twayne, 1996.

---. Preface. *A. S. Byatt*. By Kelly. New

York: Twayne, 1996. vii-xiii.

Ostriker, Alicia Suskin. *Stealing the Language: The Emergence of Women's Poetry in America.* Boston: Beacon, 1986.

Shinn, Thelma J. *"What's in a Word?" Papers on Language & Literature: A Quaterly Journal for Scholars and Critics of Language and Literature.* 31.1-2 (1995): 164-183.

Notes

i "The Riddle of Correspondences in A. S. Byatt's Possession: A Romance and H. D.'s Trilogy." *Storytelling*. Vol. 5 No. 4, Summer 2006, Washington: Heldref Publications, 223-34.

ii. Kelly's book offers information about Byatt's oeuvre that provides a foundation, based on the critical consensus about it, for more investigative study of *Possession* despite a curious consistent error in the misspelling of Roland Mitchell's [sic] name. Byatt spells it Michell.

iii. Thelma J. Shinn suggests that Christabel "bears a strong resemblance to Rossetti" and Ash to Charles Algernon Swinburne, who has written a poem entitled "The Garden of Proserpina" as did Browning.

iv. The word "threshold" begins to mirror refractions in the novel's fictional texts with H. D.'s placement of Mary Magdala in Kaspar's doorway reflecting the position of the reader on the threshold of reality and fiction once he/she subscribes to the idea of the riddle of the H. D. allusion contained within the novel's fictional riddles.

v.The literary allusions evoke the actual literary past contained within the fictional literature discussed in the novel, consequently, providing a pedagogical resource within critical studies of the novel.

vi.Thelma J. Shinn's article "What's in a Word?" discusses aspects of the relationship between the ideas of possessing knowledge and Roland's theft of the letters, p. 175. *Trilogy* refers to the thief forgiven by Christ on Golgotha in correlation to Mary Magdalene's elevation of status from sinner to forgiven due to her possession of the knowledge of Christ's forgiveness and the opportunity to exercise her faith.

vii.Leonora Stern accuses Professor Cropper of stealing Edgar Allen Poe's pawned tie-pin from an archival collection on p. 525.

viii.Kelly quotes Byatt as saying: "Greedy reading made me want to write, as if this were the only adequate response to the pleasure and power of books" in *A. S. Byatt*, p. 1.

ix.A memoir of H. D.'s correspondence with Ezra Pound entitled *End to Torment* was published by New Directions in 1979. It includes "Hilda's Book": a collection of Pound's poems for H. D.

x. The novel's connection of the LaMotte/Ash correspondence reveals that LaMotte's ideas influenced Ash's poetry, which is similar to the under-recognized contribution of H. D. to Pound's writing.

xi. Neither her husband Richard Aldington nor Ezra Pound were the father of H. D.'s daughter.

xii. Among less significant biographical tidbits supporting the idea that Byatt built in a mystery connection to H. D. for the reader to uncover is the astrological birth sign of Virgo shared by both authors. Virgo is ruled by the planet Mercury, named after the Greek god Hermes.

xiii. The multiple implications in the word "correspondence" include the following: correspondences between two texts; communication in letters; corresponding information; correspondence of text to reality.

xiv. Shinn points out that Emily Dickenson shares "an addiction to this form of punctuation" (dots or dashes) with

Christabel, p. 181.

xv. Compare H. D.'s use of the alabaster jar containing a riddle to the Byatt passage excerpted from Christabel's letter quoted earlier.

xvi. Compare H. D.'s use of this image with the thirsty man in Christabel's poem, "The Fairy Melusina."

xvii. The italics are H. D.'s. Byatt uses italics to distinguish the letters from other portions of the text.

xviii. The crown idea is paralleled in *Possession* to the Queen of the Drowned City, p. 453, and echoed in the crown of woven flowers Ash weaves for his daughter May in the "Postcript."

xix. H. D.'s sudden, unexplained time conflations predate the popular adoption of that technique by a variety of postmodern artists in narrative disciplines: some examples include playwright Tom Stoppard's *Arcadia* and film director Quentin Tarantino's *Pulp Fiction*.

xx. The train ride beginning on p. 300 can be about either couple for a substantial number of pages and is a good example of how Byatt uses the reader's confusion to superimpose her characters in the reader's mind. This is the same technique H. D. uses to accomplish similar ends.

xxi. In *Trilogy*, H. D. extends the etymology of the name Sophia, wisdom, to the SS, Spiritus Sanctus, and contrasts the initials to the lack of wisdom in the Nazi SS. *Trilogy* was written in London during World War II.

xxii. The female line can mean women's literature, which makes the absence of H. D.'s *Trilogy* from the list of literary allusions to male authors in *Possession* striking on a political level, especially when it contains so many similarities. I assume this to be a subtle clue pointing to the riddle of correspondences between the two texts.

xxiii. Michael Hardin's article "H.D.'s *Trilogy*: Speaking Through the Margins" offers a more detailed discussion of the wordplay in the poem.

[xxiv]xxiv. The few additional connections in

the notes indicate that there are more to be uncovered, but it does not purport to be close to an exhaustive list.

Other Critical Articles by Hedwig Gorski

Sin and Punishment in Chaucer's Catholic Church Then and Now

Wisława Szymborska: Some Geographic Origins of a Postmodern Psyche

Filming the Sound of Demanding Words

Collected Essays and Reviews

Jadzia Books is proud to publish the poetry, prose, and art from Dr. Hedwig Gorski's inventive and awarded genius to keep her significant oeuvre available for the public and academia. We are searching for early copies or original artifacts to create as complete an archive as possible of extant materials. Secondary materials about her work, including unpublished manuscripts, are also being solicited for possible publication. Please contact us if you want to contribute to this effort or are interested in learning more.

Contact HGDGarts@gmail.com to connect with the author or publisher, request desk and review copies, or purchase books for classes with a teacher/student discount; to schedule author appearances, readings, lectures, or interviews, etc., email first.

Jadzia Books
1053 McVeigh Road
Arnaudville, Louisiana 70512
United States

Great books for every reader

with a taste for big images and ideas

Made in the USA
Columbia, SC
04 March 2025